LeBron

A Little Golden Book® Biography

By Shasta Clinch
Illustrated by Kingsley Nebechi

A GOLDEN BOOK • NEW YORK

Text copyright © 2024 by Shasta Clinch
Cover art and interior illustrations copyright © 2024 by Kingsley Nebechi
All rights reserved. Published in the United States by Golden Books, an imprint of Random
House Children's Books, a division of Penguin Random House LLC, 1745 Broadway,
New York, NY 10019. Golden Books, A Golden Book, A Little Golden Book, the G colophon,
and the distinctive gold spine are registered trademarks of Penguin Random House LLC.
rhcbooks.com
Educators and librarians, for a variety of teaching tools, visit us at RHTeachersLibrarians.com
Library of Congress Control Number: 2023945555
ISBN 978-0-593-70830-9 (trade) — ISBN 978-0-593-70831-6 (ebook)
Printed in the United States of America
10 9 8 7 6 5 4 3 2 1

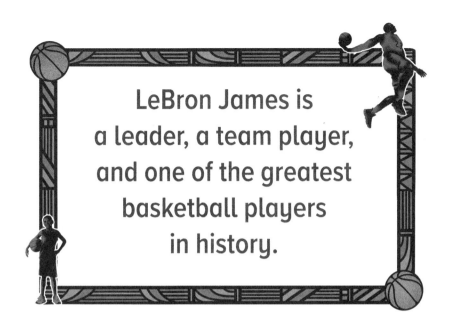

LeBron James is
a leader, a team player,
and one of the greatest
basketball players
in history.

LeBron Raymone James was born on December 30, 1984, in Akron, Ohio. He was raised by his mother, Gloria. LeBron and his mother didn't always have enough money to pay for food or a place to live. But Gloria worked hard to take care of LeBron, and she made sure he always felt loved.

LeBron and his mom moved around a lot, so he had to change schools often. This made it hard for him to focus on schoolwork and make new friends. Instead, he kept quiet and stayed in the background.

But that all changed when he was in fourth grade—LeBron started playing sports.

One day, a youth football coach named Bruce Kelker
came to LeBron's neighborhood. He was looking for
new players for his team, the East Dragons.

Coach Kelker asked all the kids to run a race. The
winner would be the team's running back. LeBron was
the fastest. He beat everyone!

LeBron loved playing football, and he was great at it, too. That first year, he scored twenty touchdowns!

Gloria volunteered as the team mom. She went to every practice, took attendance, and refilled water bottles. Most importantly, she got to watch LeBron play. She was his biggest fan.

But life was still hard for LeBron and his mom. When Coach Kelker learned that they had to move from their home again, he let them stay with him for a while.

Soon after, another coach offered to help. Frank Walker, a basketball coach, let LeBron live with him and his family. At the Walkers' house, LeBron had chores to do every day. He had to finish his homework before practice. And he always had to try his best.

Having a steady home helped LeBron. By the time he was in fifth grade, he was a star student.

When football season ended, LeBron turned to basketball. Coach Walker taught him how to dribble, shoot, and pass. He was a natural!

LeBron joined the local youth basketball team, the Shooting Stars. The players were like a family to him. He learned that working as a team was an important part of winning. The Shooting Stars made it all the way to the Youth National Championships!

LeBron and three of his teammates were known as the Fab Four. They were best friends. They even decided to go to the same high school together so they could keep playing as a team.

In high school, they won the state championships three years in a row. During LeBron's sophomore year, he was named Ohio's Mr. Basketball—the best high school player in the state! He won the title two more times.

LeBron was a great scorer, but what made him stand out was that he was a great passer, too. He always worked hard to give his teammates a chance to shine.

When he was seventeen years old, LeBron was on the cover of *Sports Illustrated* magazine. Famous pro basketball players like Michael Jordan and Shaquille O'Neal came to watch him play. People all over the country knew his name. Some even called him King James.

LeBron was now a famous basketball player, but he was still a high school student. He kept up his grades and spent time with his friends. And he stayed humble. That means he never thought he was better than anyone else. LeBron always remembered to work hard and be a team player.

LeBron always dreamed of playing for the National Basketball Association, so after high school, he entered the NBA draft. LeBron was the first player picked—by the Cleveland Cavaliers, his hometown team!

In his first season, he was named NBA Rookie
of the Year. He was the youngest player ever to get
that honor.

LeBron led the Cavaliers to the NBA playoffs every year, but they never won a championship. After seven years, LeBron left Ohio to play for the Miami Heat in Florida. Leaving his hometown team was a tough decision, but LeBron wanted a chance to win a championship ring.

In 2012, LeBron's dream finally came true. The Miami Heat beat the Oklahoma City Thunder to win the NBA championship!

The Heat won again the following year. Then, LeBron decided to go back to Ohio. He wanted to win a championship with his hometown team. And in 2016, he did! The Cavaliers won their very first NBA championship, and LeBron was named MVP— Most Valuable Player.

After four years with the Cavaliers, LeBron moved again, this time to California to play with the Los Angeles Lakers. In 2020, the Lakers won the championship, and LeBron was named MVP.

LeBron is still going strong. In 2023, he scored his 38,388th point! This made him the all-time leading scorer in NBA history. They paused the game, and Kareem Abdul-Jabbar, who held the record for nearly thirty-nine years, handed him the game ball. The crowd went wild!

LeBron has also played for Team USA in the Olympics. In 2004, he helped them win a bronze medal in Athens, Greece, and a gold medal in Beijing, China, in 2008. They won a gold medal again in London, England, in 2012.

LeBron married his high school sweetheart, Savannah Brinson, in 2013. They have three kids, Bronny, Bryce, and Zhuri.

LeBron never forgets how hard his mother worked to help him achieve his dreams. LeBron is always there for his kids and is their biggest fan!

LeBron is a world-famous athlete. But he is also a role model. He uses his fame to help make people's lives better. He and his mother started the LeBron James Family Foundation to help kids who grew up like him. In 2018, he opened a public school in his hometown called the I Promise School.

LeBron supports causes he believes in, like the power of voting. He speaks out against racism. Some people think he should focus only on basketball—but LeBron disagrees. He knows that using his voice is important. "I mean too much to so many kids that feel like they don't have a way out," he said.

LeBron James is considered one of the best basketball players of all time. But he is more than an amazing athlete. LeBron is an inspiration for people everywhere. He works hard to support his team, his family, and his community, showing the world how much he cares—both on and off the court.